Fact or Fantasy?

Reading comprehension

Brotherton Library

Isn't it enough to see that a garden is beautiful without having to believe that there are fairies at the bottom of it too?
Douglas Adams

Contents and Acknowledgements

Using this booklet

The articles are intended for silent reading. The questions can be answered both orally and in writing. They provide an opportunity for both pair and group work.

Introduction

This is a new edition of a compilation of consumer education topics first published in 1975 compared with the situation now. The world has changed: there was no broadband, personal computers or internet then; thanks to the internet there has been a huge increase in fraud and financial scams.

There is one similarity between 1975 and now: the economic situation was bad, unemployment was high and many people were having a hard time: there was an upsurge in campaigns which traded on the gullibility of the consumer,

In 1975 advertising was hardly controlled and extravagant claims for products were possible; the situation is better now but it is still possible to exaggerate the qualities of such things as health products indirectly and stay within the law: homeopathy and fad diets find a ready market; it still seems possible to slim by eating and be cured by placebos.

There has been a surge in adolescent record breakers, climbing mountains and sailing solo round the world: the rewards are great and there is always a book to be sold; the risks are great too and it's only a matter of time before some teenage adventurer comes to grief.

This compilation of items from the past and the present will allow readers to make comparisons, express opinions and perhaps be more discriminating in not accepting what they read at face value. It should be particularly useful to students as an addition to their general reading.

1 The Loch Ness Monster

When summer comes round newspaper editors turn to stories to spice up their publications in the absence of factual news: one of their favourites is Nessie, the Loch Ness Monster.

In 1975 the situation was no different. When Pearson Philip's article appeared in *The Observer* many people thought that scientists had finally solved the mystery. Here is an extract: **Nessie really does exist – official**

An international gathering of scientists will meet in Edinburgh next month to solve at last the hundred year old riddle of the Loch Ness Monster. They will have photographic evidence collected by an American research team last June which will put one matter beyond any further doubt: there is a genuine family of animals behind all the legends and the sightings.

Sir Peter Scott, the naturalist, who is one of the organisers, said last night: 'I am convinced that the Loch Ness Monster exists.' Of the photographic evidence he said: 'The most important thing shown is a flipper; there is no known whale or dolphin which has one like this.' He declined to describe the head, adding: 'It is a very strange creature.' He believed there were between twenty and fifty animals in the Loch, possibly each forty feet long.

The man credited with solving the mystery is an American physicist turned lawyer, Dr Robert Rines; he has been making a scientific investigation of Loch Ness since 1971.

The Edinburgh conference never did take place: when the photographs were released (at

£200 per copy) they were very unclear. Dr John Sheals of the Natural History museum said there was no evidence that any of the photographs were of the same object, let alone a living animal. The mystery continues.

Beyond doubt

Here is an extract from a BBC report of April 2010: A police officer believed the existence of the Loch Ness Monster was beyond doubt, according to a historical document.

In 1938 the Chief Constable of Inverness raised concerns about protecting Nessie from hunters; in a letter he wrote: 'That there is some strange creature in Loch Ness now seems beyond doubt.' The document has been released by the National Archive of Scotland as part of an exhibition.

Reports of the beast date back to 565 AD when St Columba was said to have encountered a strange water beast. Alleged sightings gathered pace in the 1930s with a series of grainy photographs of the monster appearing in newspapers. In 1933 the Scottish Office was asked to confirm the existence of a monster or sea serpent in Loch Ness. A parliamentary question was tabled in the House of Commons asking whether, in the interests of science, an investigation should be launched into the creature's existence but the question was ridiculed by the press at the time.

Ministers and civil servants were sceptical but the documents show that consideration was given to issues such a stationing observers round the Loch to capture Nessie on camera and whether it would be possible to trap the monster without injury. In the end it was felt that as the creature was popular with the public it would be better not to kill either it or the myth. However this did not stop hunters from flocking to Loch Ness in the hope of capturing the monster.

The official Loch Ness Monster site

The official site keeps readers up to date on reports of the fabled beast; in one of the latest a young couple accidentally took a photo of Nessie.

Ian and Tracey who were enjoying a weekend in the Highlands believe they may have had a close encounter with the Loch Ness Monster. Experts are now investigating the latest photograph to establish if it is in fact the Loch's most famous resident.

On their way to the cottage where they were staying, at about 11 pm they pulled into a lay-by; while they were stopped they heard a splash in the nearby Loch: 'It sounded as if a car had landed in the water,' said Ian. They used the flash on their digital camera to see where to tread on the rocks; they called out but there was no answer. On examining the photos on their camera there was one of a shape in the Loch: they believe it was Nessie.

Tourist attraction

In an article about Loch Ness the *Christian Science Monitor* wrote: 'There is, of course, a strong economic incentive to protect monsters like Nessie: tourism. Loch Ness is the main tourist attraction in the Scottish Highlands; it's a beautiful lake but tourists come from all over the world hoping for a glimpse of the famous monster. The irony is that a dead monster may be the only way to prove these creatures exist, if indeed they do.'

Questions

1 David Attenborough said on TV: 'No one could doubt the sincerity of Dr Rines or Peter Scott or that their monster pictures were genuine'. Do you agree?

2 Sir Peter Scott named the beast Nessiteras Rhombopterix, an anagram of 'Monster hoax by Sir Peter S'. Is this significant?

3 Could there be any reason for faking photographs of the monster?

4 What do you think of the Ian and Tracey story? The photograph is too vague to be recognisable as a living creature, so why report it?

5 Why are the Scottish tourism organisations keen on the Loch Ness Monster reports?

6 What would finally prove the existence of the Loch Ness Monster? Is it possible to prove that the monster does not exist?

2 The Yeti, yet again

In 1933 a newspaper reporter spotted large footprints on the shore of Loch Ness; a hoaxer made them with a hippo foot ash tray. Evidence of the existence of the Abominable Snowman or Yeti also comes mainly from photographs of footprints found in the Himalayan snow. Every few years the story is revived in newspapers; this article appeared in *Reveille* in December 1975.

The night the Yeti called

Two American scientists have returned from an expedition to the Himalayas with remarkable evidence that the Abominable Snowman, the Yeti, really exists. 'We photographed footprints in the snow that could only have been made by the Yeti,' said zoologist Dr Edward Cronin.

Dr Cronin was accompanied by Dr Howard Emery, a physician and zoologist, and two Sherpa guides. The expedition was sponsored by the World Wildlife Fund and the British Museum. When the team reached a height of 12,000 feet, they camped for the night. 'At dawn, the next morning, Howard stepped out of the tent first,' said Dr Cronin. 'He called out to me: Come here, Ted; look at these tracks; I can't believe it.'

The scientists photographed the tracks before the sun melted them and then tried to follow them; however they disappeared on rocks. Dr Cronin said, 'We discounted the possibility of a hoax, realising that the Sherpas were not capable of making the full trail of prints that we could see; they wouldn't have had the time and we doubted their ability to make prints which so closely matched the Yeti footprints we had seen in other photos.' The Yeti prints were nine inches long and nearly five inches wide; the stride was short, often less than a foot, and the scientists believed the creature used a slow cautious step.

They stayed the next three nights under the bright Himalayan moon but there was no return visit. However, during their years in Nepal they have talked to enough natives who have seen Yetis to come to this conclusion: 'The Yeti is a stocky ape-like animal that walks upright like a man; it stands about six feet tall and has short coarse reddish brown or black hair sometimes with white patches on its chest. The face is flat and hairless, the jaw strong with large teeth; the head comes to a pointed crown and the arms reach almost to the knees. Our findings suggest that the Yeti favours the dense vegetation of the steep valleys and uses the snow passes to get from one valley to the next,' said Dr Cronin.

Still hunting

This is based on a *National Geographic* article: Reinhold Messner has spent his life redefining the possible: in 1978 he defied the accepted boundaries of the human body, climbing Everest without oxygen, possibly the greatest Alpine feat of all time; he went on to climb all fourteen of Earth's 8,000 metre peaks, another record. Now he's made a study of the Yeti, yanking the Abominable Snowman into the realm of fact. He didn't believe in a real creature behind the Yeti; he had seen footprints from the 50s 60s and 70s but he never thought much about them; he said, 'It's all nonsense.'

When he saw a Yeti for himself in 1986, he thought, 'What's that?' But he couldn't see colours or a face; he could only see a shadow because it was very late. When he approached the place where the Yeti stood, he found footprints exactly like the ones they photographed in the 50s; they looked like those of a two legged animal. Much later he found out that a Tibetan bear especially on rocky or snowy ground puts its back foot in the footprints of the forefoot so that two footprints appear as one.

Mystery solved?

The Yeti is the sum of many repetitions of the legend; the local people have a lot of fantasy creatures because they live without television or Hollywood so they create their own myths but most of these myths, like the Yeti, are built on real animals.

The local people tell each other the story and from time to time somebody brings along a new part because they've been in touch in the night with one of these creatures; so the Yeti is really a Tibetan bear: the legend and the Tibetan bear match.

A dangerous animal

The legends all describe the Yeti as eight feet tall; if it's big they say it is black; if it's small they say it's reddish, because the small Tibetan bears are reddish. They all say, when the Yeti is whistling, run away because it's becoming dangerous. It stands on two legs when it meets people to show that it is big, strong and dangerous. It is able to kill a yak with one hand; no other animal can do this in the Himalayas; a yak is as big as a buffalo.

Messner says he found a dead yak killed with one hand by the Yeti or by a Tibetan bear; he did not see how it was killed but he saw first the footprints of the yak and the following footprints of a huge Yeti; afterwards he found the dead animal. The Yeti killed the yak and put it underground to store the meat like a bear would.

Questions

1 Why is the Yeti story revived every few years?
2 Why do organisations like the World Wildlife Fund and the British Museum spend considerable sums of money sponsoring expeditions to find a Yeti?
3 Could the Sherpas have made the footprints that Dr Cronin saw?
4 How was Dr Cronin able to describe the Yeti and its favoured location?
5 What is Reinhold Messner's greatest achievement?

6 Did Messner believe the Yeti existed?

7 What evidence did Messner collect about the existence of the Yeti?

8 What did he say the Yeti really was?

9 Why did he go on to say that a Yeti could kill a yak with one hand?

10 What would it take to convince you that the Yeti exists?

3 Snappy thoughts

Photography has been used and abused ever since it was invented; with the development of the digital camera anything is possible.

A famous French plumber and faith healer of the 1930s called Henaux refused to be photographed on the grounds that his face would not leave an imprint on the negative.

In 1968 an American called Ted Serios became famous as a result of his ability to think pictures on to a photographic negative; his fame faded somewhat when he was unable to do the same under controlled conditions.

Versatile Uri Geller the famous illusionist is more photogenic: unlike Henaux his face leaves an imprint on a negative even when the lens cap is left on the camera.

Fairy photographs

Douglas Adams wrote science fiction but he was a rational thinker; he said: Isn't it enough to see that a garden is beautiful without having to believe that there are fairies at the bottom of it too?

In the 1820 edition of the *Strand Magazine,* Sir Arthur Conan Doyle, the creator of Sherlock Holmes, and Edward Gardner, a psychic researcher, published pictures of two girls playing with fairies. Elsie Wright and her cousin Frances Griffiths said that they had taken the pictures at the bottom of their garden in Cottingley, Yorkshire. When the pictures were published most people thought that they had been faked; a few people however wrote to the magazine saying that they had seen fairies like those in the photographs.

Confession

In 1983 Frances and Elsie, then 75 and 81 years old, confessed that 'the fairy photographs were actually drawings that Elsie had made, cut out and set in place with hatpins'. The cut-outs were traced from 'Princess Mary's Gift Book' backed with cardboard and arranged at the bottom of the garden. Although the house was searched nothing was ever found: the book sat on a shelf unread since the time it was awarded and the girls weren't telling.

The confession was released in an article in *The Times* on 9th April 1983 in the same year in which Frances published a book in which she wrote: 'I'm fed up with all these stories: I hated the photographs and cringe every time I see them. I thought it was a joke but everyone else kept the story going; it should have died a natural death sixty years ago.' The book renewed public interest in the fairy photographs and Frances was commissioned to write an article in *The Times* newspaper. Many miles away in New Zealand, the last surviving member of Doyle's investigation team, Edward Gardner, hears the truth about the Cottingley fairies at the age of 96.

Tourism

Cottingley is a small village situated in the Aire Valley between Shipley and Bingley. Gentle streams can be seen running through the village and if followed lead you to the River Aire. The village's main claim to fame is the fairy photographs and visitors can see the house where Elsie Wright lived. She and Frances spent many hours playing in the attic bedroom and on one occasion traced images of fairies which they later photographed using Mr Wright's camera. The stream which provided the mystical backdrop to the fairy photos is only a few yards away beyond the back garden.

In 1986 Frances died aged 78 still believing in fairies; she admitted that the photos were faked but insisted that she really did see them. Her cousin Elsie with whom she had captivated the generations died in 1988 aged 84.

Questions

1 What do Henaux, Serios and Geller have in common?

2 Did Conan Doyle and Edward Gardner really believe the photos were genuine?

3 What did most people think about the fairy photos? Were they right?

4 Why did Frances and Elsie not confess the truth about the photos when they were girls?

5 Why did they wait decades before confessing?

6 Why are the fairies important to the village of Cottingley?

7 Why did Frances cringe every time she saw the photos?

8 Frances confessed that the photos were fake but insisted that she really did see the fairies. Why?

9 Who believes in fairies these days? Do you?

4 I told you so

Before Russian space probes landed on Venus, most astronomers thought the planet was like the moon: a rock-strewn desert with mountains and large craters filled with dust. They thought that, like the moon, Venus was a dead planet.

The following is a report from *The Guardian* of 27 October 1975: The Soviet Union's successful landing of two craft carrying instruments is said to have produced evidence that Venus appeared to be a live planet where rocks seemed to be thousands of years younger than those on Earth. The young appearance of the rocks testified to a comparatively recent volcanic eruption and the planet could still be alive inside.

The following is taken from an article by Peter Vane in the *Sunday Express* of 2 November 1975: The grand old man of professional star-gazing, Dr Immanuel Velikovsky was sitting alone in his attic when I telephoned. 'You are,' he said, 'the first person to take the trouble to ask me how I feel about being right about Venus. Well, I'll tell you: tremendous. I never had any doubt that I was right.' And the man who a quarter of a century ago was called 'a fraud' and 'cheap self-publicist' chuckled as he added, 'At last it's my turn to laugh.'

At 82 the doctor who is not a scientist or even an astronomer, but a psycho-analyst, is full of enthusiasm, He wrote about Venus in 1950 in his book *Worlds in Collision* to which established scientists reacted with a flood of scorn. The late Professor Haldane, one of the most brilliant of British scientists said: 'I conclude that this book is fiction.'

What were the predictions which were ridiculed by the world's leading scientists in 1950?
1 Venus is a young living planet: the Russian probes established that.
2 It probably revolves in a direction opposite to that of the other planets: a radiometric monitor in Washington proved the star-gazer was right.
3 Venus was exceedingly hot, probably somewhere near 600 degrees Fahrenheit. Again the experts laughed saying that the planet's temperature was not much above that of the average living room. Once again the doctor was proved right: in 1967 the Soviet space probe Venus 4 was sending back the indisputable fact that the temperature was 536 degrees Fahrenheit.

Dr Velikovsky spent nine years of research on his book, studying the world's oldest documents: the Old Testament, the Hindu Vedas, Babylonian tablets, Greek mythology and the Mexican annals. He said, 'I stick to my belief that our ancestors were telling the truth; the

Bible for example is not fiction: it just needs sifting, analysing, understanding and believing,'

Venus latest

Europe's Venus Express spacecraft made its rendezvous with our nearest planetary neighbour in April 2005 to study it from orbit. The mission aimed to shed light on an enduring mystery about this world: how a planet similar to our own in size, mass and composition has evolved so differently over the last 4.6 billion years.

Venus has undergone runaway greenhouse warming, trapping solar radiation; this has heated the planet's surface to an average of 872F, hot enough to melt lead. The atmosphere composed chiefly of carbon dioxide generates a surface pressure ninety times greater than that on earth.

Venus was born with the same sorts of constituents as Earth which means there was some water in the environment; some more probably came from comets. What water there was has long since boiled away: runaway greenhouse warming has left Venus one of the driest places in the Solar System.

The greenhouse effect on Venus has been driven along by volcanism: active volcanoes would have pumped copious quantities of the greenhouse gas, carbon dioxide, into the atmosphere. Water evaporating from the surface would have acted with carbon dioxide to trap solar radiation and heat up the planet.

The future

Scientists have no way of telling how long present day conditions have existed on Venus. According to one theory the current surface temperature might be stabilised through interaction between the atmosphere and minerals in the rocks. If this idea is discarded and one assumes that the greenhouse warming is driven by volcanism then conditions could be fluctuating on a relatively short timescale.

At some point volcanism will run out; it ran out on Mars a long time ago and it has partially run out on Earth. The volcanism will eventually subside to the point where it can't maintain these high temperatures. It's interesting to imagine what can happen then: recent atmospheric models predict that the harsh conditions on

Venus will eventually relax and the planet will become more like Earth.

Questions

1 Why were the results of the Venus probes a surprise to scientists?
2 What does Velikovsky mean when he says: Venus is a live planet?
3 How does Velikovsky do his research?
4 Some scientists have called Velikovsky a fraud. What do you think?
5 What happened to Venus could be a warning to Earth: in what way?
6 Could Venus become what Earth is like now? Why?

5 Venusians

In 1950 Velikovsky said that Venus was a living planet. In 1951 Frank Scully said that there were living beings on Venus. In his book *Behind the Flying Saucers* he said that they came from Venus: the saucers were made of very hard metal, were driven by magnetic propulsion and could travel faster than light. Scully said that one of the Venusian saucers had crashed; the Air Force had taken it way and found six bodies in it. These Venusians were three feet tall and when alive wrote in pictures, ate food wafers and drank heavy water.

Velikovsky never claimed that there were living beings on Venus; however he did believe that a shower of burning oil fell on Earth from the comet which became Venus; he called it star oil.

Celestial pinball

Velikovsky got his facts from the Bible and the legends of many lands. In his book *Worlds in Collision* he described how Venus was made:

1 Jupiter collided with Saturn and a piece of Jupiter became a comet.
2 The comet collided with Earth several times causing earthquakes, floods and meteor showers.
3 The comet collided with Mars and knocked it from its orbit.
4 Mars came near the Earth and caused floods and earthquakes.
5 The comet collided with Mars again near the Earth and knocked it back into orbit.

6 The comet settled into an orbit to become a planet; we call that planet Venus.

Velikovsky say that all this happened about 3000 years ago and caused the Old Testament miracles. The Bible says that Pharoah refused to let Moses' people go so God sent ten plagues to Egypt. This is the list with Velikovsky's explanations:

1 Rivers of blood: red dust fell from the comet's tail and turned the rivers red.

2 and 3 Boils and lice in men and plague in cattle: caused by the comet.

4, 5, 6 and 7 Frogs, lice, flies and locusts: all fell from the comet's tail.

8 Hailstones: meteorite showers from the comet's tail together with a shower of burning oil.

9 Darkness fell upon the Earth: the comet's gravity either stopped the Earth rotating or pulled it on to a new axis.

10 The deaths of the first born in Egypt: caused by earthquakes.

Other events

1 God gave the Ten Commandments to Moses: the comet caused an earthquake on Mount Sinai and Moses heard the Commandments in the noise.

2 The parting of the Red Sea: caused by the gravitational pull of the comet.

3 Manna sent to Moses' people in the wilderness: precipitate of carbohydrates fell from the comet's tail.

Aliens are dangerous

Just when we thought it would be nice to make the acquaintance of beings from another planet like the Venusians, Stephen Hawking issues a warning:

Aliens are out there but could be too dangerous for humans to interact with them. Intelligent alien life forms almost certainly exist but communicating with them could be too risky. They might exist in massive ships having used up all the resources of their home planet. Such advanced aliens could become nomads looking to colonise any planets they can reach.

A visit by aliens to Earth might be like Columbus arriving in the Americas which didn't turn out very well for the Native Americans. Hawking speculated that extra-terrestrial life would be like microbes or small animals. Microbial life might exist beneath the Martian surface where there is thought to be water; marine creatures might exist beneath the ice on Europa, a moon of Jupiter.

When we consider the worlds beyond the Solar System the odds in favour of life's existence rise; the numbers alone make thinking about aliens perfectly rational: the challenge is to work out what aliens might be like.

War of the Worlds

The idea of alien invasion of the Earth is common in books and films. In 1898 H G Wells published *The War of the Worlds*; this powerful story about the world being invaded by Martians made a great impression on readers. When Orson Welles broadcast a radio play version of the story in 1938 it was so realistic that there was panic in the streets of America.

Water on an asteroid

Scientists have detected water on the surface of an asteroid. The observation was made on 24 Themis a huge rock that orbits almost 480 km out from the Sun. Ice is not stable in such circumstances and has to be replenished perhaps from the inside the object. The discovery backs up the theory that much of the water in the Earth's oceans was delivered from space. It has been suggested that water on Earth may have come from impacts with many asteroids in its history; the detection of ice on an asteroid supports that idea.

Questions

1 Reports of flying saucers are frequent. Do you think Earth has been visited by alien spaceships?
2 How likely is the story of a crashed saucer with six dead aliens in it?
3 Comets brought many minerals to Earth. Is Velikovsky's theory about 'star oil' credible?
4 Are Velikovsky's explanations of Biblical events believable?
5 Why could aliens be dangerous? Would they treat us like Columbus treated the Indians?

6 Have you ever been scared by a radio broadcast, TV or film? Which ones?

7 How does the last story 'Water on an asteroid' support one of Velikovsky's theories?

6 Young Earth, Old Earth

Archbishop Ussher was a 17th century Anglican clergyman who calculated that the Earth was 6000 years old. He arrived at this figure by adding up Biblical ages and dates. This was generally accepted by Christians at the time and by many since. This is the chronology drawn up by Archbishop Ussher:

4004 BC: Creation
2348 BC: Noah's flood
1921 BC: God's call to Abraham
1491 BC: The Exodus from Egypt
1012 BC: Founding of the temple in Jerusalem
586 BC: Destruction of Jerusalem by Babylon and the beginning of the Babylonian captivity
4 BC: Birth of Jesus

Having established the first day of creation as Sunday 23 October 4004 BC, Ussher calculated the dates of other Biblical events for example:

1 Adam and Eve were driven from Paradise on Monday 10 November 4004 BC

2 The Ark touched down on Mount Ararat on Wednesday 5 May 2348 BC

Ussher was probably influenced by the widely held belief that the Earth's potential life was 6,000 years: 4,000 years before Christ and 2,000 years after. This corresponded to the six days of Creation on the grounds that 'one day is with the Lord as a thousand years and a thousand years as one day' (2 Peter 3:8); this idea has been almost completely abandoned but today some biblical scholars as well as a number of evangelical Christians believe in a literal interpretation of the Bible calling for a six thousand year old Earth.

Creation: Young Earth

The six days of Creation are:

1 Day and night separated

2 The vault of heaven (the sky) made

3 The land separated from the sea. Plants and fruit trees created.

4 The Sun and the Moon created

5 Birds and sea creatures made

6 Wild animals, cattle, reptiles and man created

Evolution: Old Earth

Modern scientists have calculated that:

1 The Sun is 4.57 billion years old

2 The Earth is 4.54 billion years old

The basic evolutionary timeline says how long ago the following appeared and looks like this:

1 Simple cells: 3.8 billion years ago

2 Photosynthesis: 3 billion years ago

3 Complex cells: 2 billion years ago

4 Multi-cellular life: 1 billion years ago

5 Simple animals: 600 million years ago

6 Arthropods (the ancestors of insects, spiders and crustaceans): 570 million years ago

7 Complex animals: 550 million years ago

8 Fish: 500 million years ago

9 Land plants: 475 million years ago

10 seeds: 400 million years ago

11 Amphibians: 360 million years ago

12 Reptiles: 300 million years ago

13 Mammals: 200 million years ago

14 Birds: 150 million years ago

15 Flowers: 130 million years ago

16 Dinosaurs died out: 65 million years ago

17 Appearance of the genus Homo: 2.5 million years ago

18 Humans started looking like they do today: 200,000 years ago

19 Neanderthals died out: 25,000 years ago

No contradiction?

The Young Earth – Old Earth positions would appear to be contradictory but in 2010 F J Ayala was awarded the Templeton Prize given to 'those who have made an exceptional contribution to affirming life's spiritual dimension'.

The professor is an authority on molecular evolution and genetics; his work may one day lead to cures for malaria and other diseases. In his view: 'There need not be contradiction between science and religion … they cannot be in contradiction because they deal in different subjects: they are like two windows through which we look at the world; the world is one and the same, but what we see is different.'

Questions

1 Was science strong in the 17th century?
2 Why did people accept Ussher's calculations?
3 Is it possible to work out such precise dates?
4 Why do many people still believe the Earth is 6.000 years old?
5 What are the Old Earth calculations based on?
6 Did man and dinosaurs live together?
7 Do you agree with Professor Ayala?

7 Faking the evidence

Piltdown man

Palaeontologists like to make their name with an amazing discovery and in the early part of the 20th century the search was on for the 'missing link', an intermediate species between apes and modern man.

When Charles Dawson, a collector, obtained fragments of a skull and jawbone in 1912 he named them after himself Eoanthropus Dawsoni,

Dawson's Dawn Man. He was told the fragments came from a gravel pit at Piltdown in England. He believed he had found the missing link and became the most famous palaeontologist of the age. It was forty years before the skull was found to be a hoax: it consisted of the lower jawbone of an orang-utan that had been deliberately combined with the skull of a fully developed modern human.

The Texas Dinosaur Beds

In the 1930s Texas was one of the states in what became known as the Dust Bowl; this resulted from poor farming methods which turned fields to dust and ruined the Texans. Desperate times called for desperate remedies so farmers looked round for some means of making money and surviving.

In what is now the Dinosaur Valley State Park there were a series of fossilised dinosaur tracks in the limestone. This unusual feature attracted visitors and gave some of the locals an opportunity to make some cash: they started cutting out the footprints and selling them to tourists. The demand was such that more footprints were needed so the farmers made them; they also had an idea for improving the tourist attraction.

Young Earth proof

It is estimated that about half the population of the USA are proponents of 'Young Earth'. They believe: the Earth is 6,000 years old; all life was created in six days; dinosaurs and man existed at the same time.

Proof of this was lacking in the fossil record so the Texas farmers provided it by carving human footprints alongside the dinosaur tracks. This was a great success: more tourists came and the stone carvers made some cash. Creationists were happy to have this proof of their 'Young Earth' beliefs.

Rewriting history

Is there such a thing as historical truth? Apparently it is possible to rewrite history to suit one's own ideas and prejudices, especially in Texas. The following information comes from an article by Chris McGreal in *The Guardian* of 17 May 2010:

Cynthia Dunbar is a Texas lawyer who sits on the Texas Education Board; along with other Christian evangelists and conservatives she is in a position to rewrite the history curriculum. She recommended:

-Ignoring Thomas Jefferson who favoured separation of church and state.

-Introducing a new focus on 'the significant contributions of pro-slavery Confederate leaders during the civil war'.

-Asserting 'the right to keep and bear arms' as an important element of a democratic society.

-Dropping the study of Sir Isaac Newton in favour of examining scientific advances through military technology.

-Dropping references to the slave trade in favour of calling it the 'Atlantic triangular trade'.

Previously Cynthia Dunbar tried to have creationism taught in science classes, calling it 'intelligent design' which is just another way of saying creationism.

Questions

1 Why would anyone fake the Piltdown skull?
2 Why did Dawson name the skull after himself?

3 Do you sympathise with the Texas farmers?

4 Why did Creationists believe the human footprints were real?

5 Is it possible to rewrite history?

6 Should church and state be separate?

7 What is the result of the right to bear arms?

8 Why does Ms Dunbar use the terms 'intelligent design' and 'Atlantic triangular trade'?

8 A real tonic

Where the bee sucks ...

Mediaeval alchemists spent their time searching for two things: the philosopher's stone and the elixir of life; the former would change base metals into gold and the latter bestow eternal life: the search for the elixir goes on.

Substances connected with the bee have always been popular health foods, perhaps it's because as one advertisement said: 'Honey is the source of energy bees need to carry their bulky bodies and the pollen they collect from flower to flower, a feat which makes our modern transport aircraft look hopelessly inadequate'.

One company's advertisement asks: 'Does pollen help to delay the onset of old age?' The advertisement doesn't say in so many words that it does but: 'Research workers in America and Russia have suggested that pollen in a diet may hold the secret of why certain bee-keeping communities enjoy a much longer average lifespan than most in our society'.

What makes pollen and honey so magical?
Honey is 76.4% sugar and 23% water;
It contains traces of several vitamins and minerals but less of these than almost any other food.
Pollen is made up of 40% carbohydrates (as in bread); 35% protein (as in meat); traces of vitamins and minerals (but less than in most foods); 10-13% amino acids (as in cheese).

Pass the iron, please
In 1950 most newspapers and magazines carried advertisements for pills, tonics and foods which contained vitamins or iron or both. The

advertisements urged us to start the day with bran flakes and iron because 'active people need plenty of iron in their diet'. One brand of vitamin and iron pills promised to allow us 'to get three days out of every weekend'; a tonic wine promised to give you 'that on top of the world feeling' which was another way of saying that it would make you drunk because it contained alcohol.

To be taken with a pinch of salt

In 1975 an advertisement for sea salt waxed lyrical and the blurb on the packet was sheer poetry: 'La Baleine Sea Salt is from the clear blue Mediterranean evaporated by sun and sea breezes; it is then washed in more sea water. You don't expect to feel as if you are just back from St Tropez when the packet is empty but if you hold it to your ear you might just hear the sea.'

Sea salt is like any other salt it just costs a bit more and the Mediterranean is so polluted that it is no recommendation that it comes from there.

Be careful what you claim

Just as they were decades ago, honey and tonics are still promoted but as an advertisement for Active Manuka Honey says: 'There have been many observed beneficial effects of using honey … but the UK Trading Standards prevents them from being talked about here.'

The advertisements may be careful not to make extravagant claims but there is more than one way to promote a product. On the Manuka Honey website you are urged 'to discover more of the specific applications of the honey and why it has proved so effective, please click on the research articles link … you will find many case studies and research articles written by the New Zealand medical establishment'.

In spite of the UK Trading Standards requirements, the advertiser still manages to say quite a lot about Manuka Honey: 'In recent years honey has begun to enjoy a renaissance in its use as a therapeutic treatment for many internal and external ailments both serious and minor. The discovery of a unique anti-bacterial property has led Manuka Honey to be considered for both external and internal digestive uses. Previously this valuable natural resource has been disregarded by conventional medical wisdom, to be regarded as no more important than any other traditional or homeopathic remedy.'

Questions

1 Does a bee have any problem flying from flower to flower?

2 How do honey merchants sell their product?

3 Does honey have magical properties?

4 Advertisements for tonic wine have disappeared. Why?

5 Manuka is a flower which grows in New Zealand and now in Britain. Cornish Manuka costs £55 a jar. Why?

6 What prevents excessive claims for the medical value of products from being advertised?

7 How do companies circumvent UK Trading Standards?

8 Do you like honey? Why?

9 Building pyramids

What are homeopathic remedies?

Homeopathic remedies are made from herb extracts diluted so much that there remains little or nothing of the original substance. One tincture is made from the reflected light from a buttercup on a great deal of water. Anyone who claims to have been cured of an illness using homeopathic remedies is experiencing what is known as the placebo effect.

What is a placebo?

In simple words if you think something is doing you good you will feel better but if you are really sick see a regular doctor.

Telling Prince Charles that homeopathic remedies are simple placebos will not please the future king; neither will the following extract from an article by Robert Booth in *The Guardian* of 27 April 2010.

An aide to Prince Charles' campaign for wider use of complementary medicine in the NHS was arrested at dawn yesterday on suspicion of fraud and money-laundering at the Prince's health charity.

The arrest follows a police investigation into £300,000 unaccounted for in the books of the charity of which the Prince is president. The foundation promotes homeopathy, herbal remedies and other complementary medicines in line with the Prince's advocacy of their wholesale application in the public health sector.

Prince Charles established the charity in 1993 to explore 'how safe proven complementary therapies can work in conjunction with mainstream medicine'. But since then his ventures in complementary medicine have been attacked in some quarters as unscientific. Edzard Ernst, professor of complementary medicine at Exeter University, described a 'Detox Artichoke and Dandelion Tincture' made by the Prince's Duchy Originals Company as 'outright quackery'.

Profits from the company have helped to fund the foundation which also received more than £1m in public funds mainly from the Department of Health since its launch in 1993 and almost £3m from the Prince's Charities Foundation which handles his personal giving.

The Commons Science and Technology Select Committee concluded that there was no evidence that homeopathy had anything other than a placebo effect and said manufacturers should no longer be allowed to make therapeutic claims.

The Prince of Wales complementary health charity ceased operating a week later.

What are pyramids made of?

Have you tasted Noni juice? It comes mainly from Tahiti; one of its names is 'vomit fruit' and it really does taste foul. However medicines are not supposed to taste nice so noni juice is sweeping the world in pyramid sales: you get agents who recruit agent who recruit agents ad infinitum and build the pyramid. Agents don't actually drink the foul potion they just sell it on to other agents.

When David Beckham joined LA Galaxy he played for a soccer team whose shirts were sponsored by Herbalife a pyramid sales organisation. The only reason to buy Herbalife products is to sell them on to other agents so building the pyramid. The company is careful not to make claims about the beneficial effects of its products; they put these in pamphlets which are only given to agents. The attraction is the commission paid to agents on the products they sell on to more agents producing commissions in ever greater amounts for the agents at the top of the pyramid.

Acai fruit

The latest fad is for acai fruit which tastes like dirt so it must be good for your health. The impoverished Amazonian Indians who collect the fruit can't believe their luck; they are selling large quantities to American companies which advertise its anti-oxidant powers; they blend the fruit into Snapple red tea and everything from dietary supplements to beauty products.

Questions

1 Homeopathic remedies have no effect. Why do people buy them? Why do Boots the Chemist sell them when they admit they are useless?
2 Why does Prince Charles promote homeopathy?

3 Why did the Department of Public Health donate money to the Prince's foundation?
4 Why do pyramid schemes prosper?
5 Should a tonic taste foul to do you good?
6 Did David Beckham know Herbalife was sponsoring LA Galaxy before he joined the club?
7 Is the UK Trading Standards Authority doing its job?

10 A powerful way to make money

When Galvani demonstrated his electrical machine in 1786 he believed he had discovered the life force; his discovery became the basis for thousands of electrical cures.

In 1795 an American, Dr Elisha Perkins, was curing rheumatism and many other complaints by drawing two metal rods across his patients. His son Benjamin came to England and treated many important people. But Dr John Haygarth of Bath painted two wooden rods to look like metal and drew them across five sufferers from rheumatism who pronounced themselves cured.

Perkins decided to go back to America having made a fortune with his two metal rods.

Fifteen years later Count Mattei of Bologna treated many important patients, including the Pope, with his remarkable electric fluid. He was very successful until the public analyst discovered that the fluid was coloured water.

In 2010 a company called BHIA promoted what they called 'Electro Homeopathy'; the remedies came in three colours: red, green and white. Their website said: 'The Italian noble Count Mattei discovered these remedies in the 1800s; being a herbalist, he prepared them from herbs and named them Electro Homeopathic medicines. In 1869 the Pope opened a ward in a Roman hospital where the remedies could be tested: the results were astonishing.'

The good old days

Some advertisements for electrical cures would not be allowed today; here is one from the 19th century:
Health, comfort and Elegance positively assured with this beautiful invention.

By a happy thought Dr Scott of London the inventor of the celebrated electric hair brush has adapted electro-magnetism to ladies' corsets, thus bringing this wonderful curative agency within the reach of every lady.

A tendency to extreme fatness or leanness is a disease which in most cases these articles will be found to cure. The secretary of the Pall Mall Electric Association of London earnestly recommends all ladies suffering from any bodily ailment to adopt these corsets without delay: they perform astonishing cures and invigorate every part of the system.

Copper bracelets

In 1975 advertisements for items that cured rheumatism were appearing in newspapers and magazines. Copper bracelets were a favourite: it used to be thought that copper from coffin handles was the best; the argument was that because the dead felt no pain the wearer of the copper bracelet felt no pain either.

Here is one advertisement by Rumaton: Millions of people have worn copper bracelets for the last fifty years; this speaks for itself. Why not wear this most attractive copper bracelet for two weeks and convince yourself; if you are not satisfied just return it for a refund: we think you'll be glad to keep it.

Magnetic copper bracelets

In 2010 there was a demand for copper bracelets especially the magnetic kind. They are now marketed as jewellery but the inference is that the magnetic part of the name will have curative properties.

Knee pads

In 1975 you could buy Rumaton impregnated knee pads 'for every man and woman suffering from muscular pain. Elasticised pure wool impregnated with the remarkable Rumaton solution retains and reflects back your body warmth and helps to promote blood circulation; these medicated garments should be worn by sufferers who dread aches and pains'.

Are we now less gullible than in Galvani's day? There are still many of companies offering cures in the form of ant-rheumatic pain plasters. Here is a typical example: 'Anti-rheumatic pain plaster is formulated from traditional Chinese medicine; Siberian ginseng has long been recognised for its effectiveness in activating and promoting blood circulation, dispersing bruises, arresting bleeding and reducing muscle inflammation and swelling; it is also an effective pain killer.'

Electrical treatments in 2010

Serious claims for electrical treatments abound; this report appeared in *The Telegraph* in 2009:

Hope for Parkinson's patients

Early research in mice and rats using electrical treatment improved the slow stiff movements associated with the disease. Experts believe if the technique works it could provide a passport to normal living for thousands of Parkinson's patients.

One radical remedy for the condition is deep brain stimulation which involves inserting electrodes deep in the brain but the treatment is costly and not suitable for everyone. The new therapy targeting the spinal cord instead of the brain would be much easier and cheaper to administer.

Professor Nicolelis who led the research said: 'We see an immediate and dramatic change in the animal's ability to function when the device stimulates the spinal cord.'

Galvani did this with a frog's legs in 1786 causing them to twitch; the only difference was that the frog was dead.

Questions

1 Were people in the 18th century particularly gullible?
2 Are people gullible now?
3 Can you believe that coloured water is still being sold as an electrical cure?
4 Why were the results in the Roman hospital 'astonishing'? Make a guess.
5 Why wouldn't the advertisement for the electric corset be allowed today?
6 Do people buy copper bracelets simply as jewellery?
7 Why did a company add the word 'magnetic' to their copper bracelets?
8 Medical procedures involving electrical current are widely researched. Have you heard of any successful cures?

11 What are little boys made of?

Vocational training

In Charles Dickens' novel *Oliver Twist* we are given a dramatic picture of boys being trained as professional criminals. In this extract innocent young Oliver realises what kind of work Fagin's boys do.

The three boys sallied out, the Dodger with his coat sleeves tucked up and his hat cocked as usual; Charlie Bates sauntered along with his hands in his pockets; Oliver between them wondering where they were going and what branch of manufacturing he would be instructed in first.

The old gentleman was a very respectable looking personage with a powdered head and gold spectacles. He had taken up a book from the stall and stood there reading away as hard as if he were in his elbow chair in his own study.

What was Oliver's horror and alarm as he stood a few paces off looking on with eyes wide open to see the Dodger plunge his hand into the old gentleman's pocket and draw from thence a handkerchief. To see him hand the same to Charlie Bates and finally behold them both running away round the corner at full speed.

In an instant the whole mystery of the handkerchiefs, and the watches, and the jewels and the Jew rushed upon the boy's mind. He stood for a moment with the blood tingling through all his veins from terror, that he felt as though he were in a burning fire; then confused and frightened he took to his heels; and not knowing what he did made off as fast as he could lay his feet on the ground.

A hundred years on

Times were hard for most people when Dickens wrote *Oliver Twist*; a hundred years later boys are better fed, better looked after and they usually get pocket money. You would not expect them to have the same incentive to steal but in the facts revealed in 1975 by William Belson's report, *Juvenile Theft,* show that the situation is just as bad as in Dickens' day.

Nine out of ten boys commit petty thefts

The report finds that nine out of ten boys steal and that by the time they leave school the average boy will have stolen a hundred times.

Why do boys steal?

The report found five major factors:
1 The belief that the police will not catch the offender
2 Truancy
3 A desire for fun and excitement
4 Association with boys already engaged in stealing
5 A lack of moral conscience where stealing was concerned
Less important factors
1 Unpleasant or unattractive homes
2 Working mothers
3 Boredom
4 Wants that exceed means
5 Early separation from mothers
What deters thieves?
1 Getting caught
2 Frequent church attendance
3 Having grandparents at home

There's nothing wrong

These figures from the report give the percentage of boys who found nothing wrong with the actions listed below:

1 Keeping something you have found.........48
2 Taking pencils from school...................29
3 Buying things you know were pinched......23
4 Pinching from someone who has plenty.....22
5 Pinching things from a big company.........15
6 Pinching things from the government........11
7 Pinching from a shop............................8
8 Robbing a bank..................................4
9 Pinching from a friend...........................1
10 Pinching from an old lady... 0

135 years on

According to this extract from a legal report, things have not changed since Dickens' day:

Statistical data shows that male youths are twice as likely to commit crimes as females. Almost every young adult commits some sort of crime during his adolescence.

Development of delinquency in young males is influenced by many factors. Some scientists believe that there is a strong link between male juvenile delinquency and traumatic experiences. These can lead to desolation and depression in male adolescents, and research indicates that loneliness and depression are a major cause of delinquency among young adults. Some studies suggest that depressed and isolated males are five times more likely to commit crimes than non-depressed male youths.

Truancy

Truancy is one of the basic factors in juvenile delinquency; truanting provides plenty of time to get into mischief. This is an extract from a *Guardian* article: In 2009 truancy was at a record high with ten million days missed. The rise came despite a tougher line by ministers on absenteeism, prosecuting 9,500 parents and fining thousands more because of their children's truancy.

Some 67,000 pupils in England skipped school without permission every day in 2008-2009, almost 2,000 more than the previous year. Primary school pupils accounted for the main increase in truancy; the rate has remained static in secondary schools.

The schools minister said higher truancy rates were the fault of parents rather than schools and that teachers no longer accepted weak excuses for pupils' absence such as over-sleeping.

Questions

1 What did the Dodger and Charlie Bates do for a living?

2 Why was Oliver shocked when the boys robbed the old man?

3 Have you read the book? Did you like it?

4 Are you surprised by the findings of the Belson report? What is the most important one?

5 Do you believe the statistics in 'There's nothing wrong'?

6 What are the commonest causes of male youth crime?

7 Is the schools minister right to blame parents rather than schools for truancy?

12 And what are little girls made of?

In a 1970 article in *The Guardian,* Eva Figes commented on the Belson Report and noted that it only considered boys; was this because of the myth that only males commit crimes? She described a day she spent in a Juvenile Court. This is an extract:

It had been arrange for me to spend a day in court because I was comparing the treatment of male and female offenders. 'Oh you can't compare them,' the lady magistrate argued, 'they commit such different offenses.' They certainly did: the girls who appeared in court that day were immeasurably more professional than the boys. While boys sheepishly admitted to having stolen a box of matches or tinkered with a parking meter, the female minority had shoplifted the entire length of Oxford Street or made generous use of a stolen cheque book before getting caught. Girls it seems have to be very bad before anybody thinks they are horrid.

The lady magistrate is not at all unusual in thinking that girls are more moral and law abiding than boys. The police believe it, spend far less time trying to catch them red handed and if they do are much more likely to let them go with a caution. When the girls become women the same chivalrous attitude applies. The statistics show that if a female does fall foul of the law she not only has a far higher chance of being sent home with a caution but that even if she is charged the chances of her getting a custodial sentence are infinitesimal. Apart from everything else a girl kept in a prison cell for one night is more likely to cause uproar in the press than a thousand forgotten boys kept under lock and key for eighteen months or more.

Even juries acquit more women, perhaps less influenced by the professional view that female criminals are sick, than by the popular one that women are incapable of organised villainy. I don't blame the sisterhood for keeping quiet about this particular form of sex discrimination, but I do think it is time sociologists stopped believing that girls are made of sugar and spice.

In 2010

This is an extract from a *Mail Online* article by Steve Doughty: Teenage girls are now more likely than boys to drink, steal and take drugs a survey has shown. In a disturbing confirmation of the spread of the 'ladette' culture, it found violence, aggression and self-destructive behaviour had spread alarmingly among girls over the last twenty years.

While boys appear less likely to be drawn towards crime than they were, social problems are stacking up among teenage girls who are now expected to compete on equal terms with boys for educational opportunity and jobs.

The study of 14 and 15 year olds was conducted in a questionnaire and the results compared with a similar one from 1985. Professor Colin Pritchard who led the research said, 'Girls now smoke and binge drink more than boys; they truant, steal and fight at similar rates. Binge drinking which was admitted by nearly a third of the girls in their early teenage years drove other anti-social behaviour.

The study found that the number of boys admitting to smoking has nearly halved to just over a quarter while the number of girls who smoke has risen to nearly half.

The research produced by academics at Bournemouth University suggested there had been an improvement in behaviour among boys. The number who admitted stealing had halved as had the number who were regularly in fights; truanting was also down

Questions

1 What was the attitude of the magistrates to girl offenders in 1970?

2 How did the treatment of girls differ from that of boys?

3 Did Eva Figes think that girls were 'made of sugar and spice'?

4 How has the behaviour of girls changed since Eva Figes wrote the article?

5 How do boys compare with girls regarding their behaviour?

6 Do you think the final article is accurate?

7 How does the situation in your area compare with the Bournemouth University findings?

13 The greyhounds and the hare

In October 1975 the House of Common passed a bill banning hare coursing. John Ezzard of *The Guardian* went to a meeting to see what happened. This is part of his article:

Coursing is a method of extermination which makes an elaborate sport out of pitting one fast elegant creature, the greyhound, against another the hare. The greyhound eats meat and is thought worth its keep as a domestic pet. The hare, wild, eats young crops and is classed by food growers as vermin.

Coursing is an end-game, its moves noted and given marks on green score cards. It finishes with the death or escape of the hare. The greyhound is a superb hunter and the hare a superb quarry. Twenty-seven of the 35 hares from the young barley of Rectory Farm got away, leaving each pair of hounds behind, broken winded, and their owners walked up to a mile through plough-land to whistle them in. Even this kill-rate was high by the standards of the Scott-Henderson report on the sport, which found an average of 20 per cent of courses ended in death.

A coursing greyhound is meant to kill with a chop of the teeth which snaps the hare's neck and then to leave the corpse un-mutilated. Sometimes the dog behind gets jealous and grabs a leg; more rarely the first dog manages to get a leg and the second dog pounces to make the kill.

This is alleged to produce the 'living rope' horror which the League Against Cruel Sports and 180 MPs believe to typify coursing. Of the six kills I was able to see at a long distance, the dogs froze as soon as one or both had the hare and waited for their owners. I asked to see four of the corpses, in three the injury was to the neck only, so clean and deep that blood hardly showed on the fur. In the fourth a leg was badly torn. It was impossible to tell whether this had happened immediately before or after the kill. I had seen nothing cruel happen – unless to chase and kill any animal is cruel.

Illegal hare coursing in 2010

A BBC investigation revealed that the Hunting Act which banned hare coursing is being flouted with as many hares dying as before the ban. Many saw it as cruel and barbaric and the ban could not have come a moment too soon. For others it was an attack on a much-loved country tradition. Hare coursing, or chasing hares across a field with greyhounds for sport was outlawed under the Hunting Act of 2004. Anyone now caught doing it faces arrest and a large fine if convicted.

'They can convict me, they can fine me, they can put me in prison, but there is no way I shall ever pack up,' said one of the hunters: he is a hare courser and proud of it. As far as he's concerned the hunting ban has made no difference to his sport. He talked candidly about how the Hunting Act is regularly flouted. 'We chase anywhere between 30 and 40 hares a day and usually a third of them will be caught.

The hunter's description of how the dogs chase, catch and kill hares will be abhorrent to many. The government brought in the Hunting Act to protect the hare which rarely stands a chance of surviving the teeth of a super-fast greyhound. The hunter explained how loopholes in the law allowed coursers to continue chasing hares. Under the Hunting Act dogs are allowed to flush out hares from undergrowth but only if it is to prevent damage to crops. The landowner has to give permission and a hare must be shot immediately it is flushed out.

The hunter takes a shotgun to make it appear that he is hunting within the law. He carries a gun in case someone sees him and reports him to the police. If the police come, he explains that he is hunting legally. So far there have been very few convictions under the Hunting Act. The police report that the act has given them increased powers but when a case comes to court most illegal coursers have been prosecuted using ancient gaming and trespassing laws.

Questions

1 Is hare coursing a sport?
2 Why are hares considered to be vermin?
3 Does a hare have a chance of escape from a greyhound?
4 Is hare coursing cruel?
5 The Hunting act banned hare coursing. Why does it continue?
6 How do coursers avoid prosecution?
7 Is it cruel to shoot hares?
8 What would you do if you witnessed hare coursing?

14 Tally-ho!

Olivia Manning, the novelist, is a very sensitive person who objects to hunting animals for sport. This is what she had to say in *The Observer Magazine* of 27 November 1975:

Oscar Wilde's description of the hunt as 'the unspeakable in pursuit of the uneatable' gives less than half of it. What the touts of the hunting field cannot conceive is the effect of their activities on people more sensitive, imaginative and vulnerable then they are.

We once had a neighbour who during the day was a normal person working in an office, but at night went hare coursing and at weekends would put on a monstrous pair of breeches and hunt the fox. She admitted that, having an indifferent seat, she did not enjoy being jolted about on a horse, she did not like the kill and she really hated the cries of a hare being torn to pieces by dogs. 'But,' she said, 'hunting and coursing are the in things and they are the only way to meet the right people.'

Simon Hoggart says

His parliamentary report in the *Guardian* of 22 October 1975 began like this:

Most of the Prime Minister's question time was devoted yesterday to rabies and the unpleasant fact that if the disease ever spreads here most of the foxes in Britain will have to be slaughtered.

It is, as the Prime Minister kept telling us, a very serious subject. Quite apart from the menace of rabies itself, nobody on the Labour side wants our foxes to disappear, partly because they have a vague feeling that foxes are in some way the sworn enemies of the landed class.

The battle goes on

Even though fox hunting with dogs was banned by law, the Hunt Saboteurs still try to impede the progress of the horses and hounds. In 2009 events took a very serious turn as reported in this extract from the *Mail Online*:

Hunt saboteur charged with murder

An animal rights activist who piloted a gyrocopter that decapitated a hunt supporter was cleared of manslaughter. Bryan Griffiths and his cameraman were trying to take off from Long Marston airfield when Trevor Morse was killed while trying to stop them; Mr Morse was a member of the Warwickshire hunt.

During the confrontation of March last year, Mr Morse stood in the way of the machine and was struck by the rear blades. Mr Griffiths was charged with manslaughter by gross negligence but yesterday a jury at Birmingham Crown court acquitted him after a two-week trial.

Mutual hatred

In spite of the fact that fox hunting with hounds was banned in 1994 the hunt saboteurs still try to disrupt hunt meetings. Reports like the following extract from a Hunt Saboteurs Association publication frequently appear:

Knocked unconscious

On 30 October a group of hunt saboteur were attacked by a gang of hunt supporters at the opening meet and one was knocked unconscious with an iron bar and ridden over by the huntsmen: six received cuts and bruises.

Simon has the last word

Before the 2010 general election many conservatives hoped that the ban on fox hunting would be lifted. The new government has much more important things to deal with so the topic has been dropped. It doesn't matter anyway because as Simon Hoggart wrote in the *Guardian*: 'Fox hunting is now illegal yet carries on much as before: in that way everyone is happy except the foxes.'

Questions

1 Do you agree with Oscar Wilde's description of fox hunting?

2 Are hunting and coursing the only way to meet the right people?

3 Is Olivia Manning's article biased?

4 Why does Simon Hoggart say that Labour feel that foxes are the sworn enemies of the landed class?

5 If fox hunting is banned why do hunt saboteurs persist in disrupting the hunt?

6 What lesson can be learnt from the death of Bryan Griffiths?

7 Why do hunt saboteurs' reports use language like 'knocked unconscious with an iron bar' and 'ridden over by a huntsman'?

8 Do you support the ban on fox hunting? Why?

15 Eat to slim

In 1971 word got round that you could slim by eating bananas or hard boiled eggs: two good ways of getting fatter. Then an American couple advertised a secret diet based on eating grapefruit. This was supposed to start the 'fat burning process'. Thousands of people paid for the secret diet and got the message: eat less of the things that make you fat. The grapefruit craze did have results: the price of the fruit soared making citrus farmers in South Africa, Israel and Cyprus very happy.

So people want to eat and slim at the same time. 'Very well,' said one company, 'We shall sell ordinary food in smaller packages and say that they are a complete meal so our customers will get thinner.'

Polly Toynbee spotted the fraud. This is an extract from an article she wrote in the *Observer*:

Slimming food that does not slim you

'Limmits provide a good natural way to slim,' says the label on the packages of Limmits slimming foods. 'Natural' is the key word: the biscuits, chocolates, soups and breakfast cereals are ounce for ounce as fattening, full of sugar, flour and fat as ordinary non-slimming products.

The only difference between the content of a bar Cadbury's Dairy Milk chocolate and that of a bar of Limmits chocolate is that Limmits has added vitamins. Another difference is the price: Cadbury's costs less than half the Limmits price; the added vitamins in Limmits cost less than 1p.

'Three complete low calorie meals' say the labels on some Limmits products. The claim is a clever one: the substances are not low calorie, they are exceptionally high calorie – but eaten in small amounts as a whole meal they do constitute a low calorie meal. They are sold in small packages – that is the difference.

A message from Naomi

In 2010 Naomi Campbell appeared to have hit on a sure-fire way of burning off those calories. Here is an extract from Alexandra Topping's article in *The Guardian* of 5 May:

In an interview with Oprah Winfrey the model shared her devotion to a diet involving drinking a cocktail of maple syrup, cayenne pepper, lemon juice and water and eating nothing else. 'I try to do this three times a year: the most I've ever done it for is 18 days; I started on Saturday so this is my sixth day,' said Naomi in a video demonstrating her workout routine. She added: 'It's good just to clean out your body once in a while.'

Anna Raymond says:

No matter what you call it, this is just a faddy, flash 'detox' which is essentially a way of starving yourself. The idea that it is good for Naomi Campbell to rid her body of toxins by doing these fasts, whether it is for six or eighteen days, is complete nonsense.

People often get headaches and feel quite ill following a detox and think it is caused by the toxins coming out of the body. This is absolute rubbish: you are getting the headaches and feeling ill because you are forcing your body to create toxins by putting it in starvation mode. Naomi Campbell's mental faculties will also be affected by such extreme diets and frankly it is quite scary that she is advocating something like this to the public.

The fresh air diet

This is an extract from an article by Rajesh Joshi:

Starving yogi astounds Indian scientists

An 83 year old Indian man who says he has spent seven decades without food and water has astounded a team of military doctors who studied him for two weeks. Prahlad Jani spent a fortnight in a hospital under constant surveillance from a team of 30 medics equipped with cameras and closed circuit television. During that period he neither ate nor drank. 'We don't know how he survives,' neurologist Sudhir Shah told reporters at the end of the experiment.

'It is a mystery; if Jani does not derive energy from food and water, he must be doing that from energy sources around him, sunlight being one.'

Questions

1 Who benefitted from the 'secret diet'?
2 Why was the advertisement for Limmits deceptive?
3 In 2010 many adopted the maple syrup, cayenne pepper, lemon juice and water diet. How do you think it tastes?
4 What are the health dangers of fasting?
5 Do you agree with Anna Raymond that Naomi's diet is dangerous?
6 Could the diet affect her mental faculties?
7 Is it possible to live for decades without food or water?

16 Man's best friend

Ever since prehistoric man tamed the wolf, pets have been central to many people's lives. More than 600 years ago, Geoffrey Chaucer wrote *The Canterbury Tales* and, in the Prologue, described the Prioress, one of the pilgrims going to the shrine of Thomas a Becket at Canterbury. Judging by the following lines, rendered in modern English, the Prioress was an early example of the long line of English pet lovers:

She was so charitable and sensitive
She would weep if she saw a mouse
Caught in a trap, whether it be dead or injured
She had some little dogs which she fed
With roast meat or finest bread and milk;
And she wept bitterly if one of them died,
Or if men hit one smartly with a stick.
She was all feeling and a tender heart.

Pampered pets in 1975

Go into any supermarket and you will find a section devoted to pet foods and accessories. This is an extract from an article in the *Observer* by Diane Fisher:

Santa Claws is back in town

Britain's pets have never had it so good. In a year when most families have had to lower their standards, the multi-million pound pet accessory trade is booming. Harrods' prize offering for

Christmas, for example, is a seven pound, two and a half feet long Chewdles beef hide shin bone which costs eleven pounds fifty. Harrods report that its pet paraphernalia turnover has more than doubled this year in contrast with other departments where sales have slumped.

Britain's 10 million cats and dogs are being brushed, clothed, treated and coddled by a host of manufacturers both here and abroad. But the manufacturer whose products have become a household word is Good Boy Pet Foods; ever since the mink clad Queen Mum was discovered returning from hospital eight years ago with a tin of Good Boy Choc Drops for her corgis, Good Boy has been a brand leader. It is owned by the 200 year old family controlled public company Armitage Brothers whose turnover on pet foods last year was nearly four million pounds.

Still pampered

Pets are still being pampered: sales of pet foods and accessories have continued to be strong. Pampered doesn't quite cover the case of Conchita: some dogs might bite an odd slipper, Conchita actually choked on her own Cartier necklace and now, Conchita, known to her family as The Boss, refuses to wear diamonds anymore because of the mishap. However her owner still spends $10,000 a month on Louis Vuitton bags, bikinis, pearls, dresses and make up for her. She has her own special pink racing car bed, bathroom and TV and lunches daily on fresh grilled chicken breasts at an exclusive club in Miami.

With weekly manicures, her own minder and a publicist, this one year old, one pound Chihuahua is living the dog life equivalent of Paris Hilton and, like the hotel heiress, Conchita's owner is the daughter of a billionaire businessman. Sadly she died recently leaving $12m to Conchita and $25m to her staff who will live rent free in the Miami beach-front mansion and take care of Conchita and two other dogs.

A sound mind in a sound doggy
Pets have mental problems too as well as their owners. This is an extract from an article by Leslie Toulson in *The Sun*:

Willie's worries

Willie is a dog under mental stress say the experts. The trouble is that Willie had a posh poodle for a mum but his dad was a Cairn terrier. His unusual behaviour started soon after his owner took him on. She says, 'He was totally unaware of what was going on around him and his eyes were funny.' She took him to a dog psychiatrist who wired his head to electrical gadgets and said, 'He's got a mental disorder.' Now every nine months Willie has to go to another specialist for an expensive jab and tranquillisers.

Questions

1 How is the Prioress typical of pet owners?
2 In a world where many people go hungry is it moral to spend so much on feeding pets?
3 In 1975 many people were in difficulty due to a bad economy. Why did sales of pet food and accessories continue to be strong?
4 Who set the fashion for pet treats?
5 Some owners spend huge amounts on their pets. Can you understand why?
6 What is your opinion of Conchita's owner?

7 Is it reasonable to pay for psychiatric treatment for a dog?

17 The happier hunting ground

In the USA a new pets' cemetery open every three months. One rich American child used to fly hundreds of miles every weekend to visit the grave of her hamster, Beanie. England also has pet cemeteries. This is an excerpt from a 1975 article in *Reveille.*

They buried Lady, the brown and white cat, in a coffin of polished agba wood in a private grave marked with a marble headstone. Next to her were 'Shu Shu Bestest Woofa in All the World' and 'Mitzi, aged 9, One of God's Dear Creatures.' They are all three buried in an animal cemetery in Sussex.

While some people might laugh and say that giving animals funerals is sentimental rubbish, the man who runs it does not agree. In fact he sees the animal graveyard as a social service. He explains: 'About 4,000 pets die every day and disposing of their bodies is a great problem. You must also not forget the place a pet occupies in the owner's life; it's not a cat or a dog that has died but a real personality.'

Famous dogs

In 2010 the number of pet cemeteries has multiplied until every town has one or more. The status of dogs in Britain is such that a *Walk of Fame* has been opened in Battersea Park. This reverence for dogs both real and fictional goes back a long way.

Greyfriars Bobby

In the 19th century, Greyfriars Bobby, a Skye Terrier, became famous in Edinburgh after spending 14 years guarding the grave of his owner, John Gray, until he died himself in 1872. A year later Lady Burdett-Coutts had a statue and fountain erected at the southern end of the George 1V Bridge to commemorate him. There were no pet cemeteries in 1872, so Bobby was buried in Greyfriars Kirkyard not far from his master's grave. Several books and films have been based on Bobby's life; the latest film *The Adventures of Greyfriars Bobby* was made in 2006.

Michiko

Hachiko, a Japanese dog, was brought to Tokyo by his master, Dr Ueno, in 1924. During the owner's life, Hachiko saw his master out of the door and greeted him at the end of the day at the nearby Shibuya railway station. This routine lasted until May 1925 when Dr Ueno did not return on his usual train; he died of a heart attack and never returned to the station where his friend was waiting. Hachiko was loyal and every day for the next nine years he waited at the station. He died on the steps where he waited for his master. In April 1934 a bronze statue of Hachiko was erected at Shibuya station.

The Dog Walk of Fame

This was opened in 2007 and the public voted for the first few inductees all but one of them were dogs who had appeared in films. The exception was Gromit a cartoon character. Hachiko was overlooked but with the making of *A Dog's Story* with Richard Gere in 2009 that may change.

Here is the initial list on the Walk of Fame:
Bullseye from *Oliver Twist*

Lassie from *Lassie Come Home*
Toto from *The Wizard of Oz*
Greyfriars Bobby
Gromit from the *Wallace and Gromit* cartoons
Chance and Shadow from *Homeward Bound*
Fang from the *Harry Potter* films

Questions

1 Have you got a pet? When it dies how will you dispose of the body?
2 Do you think pet cemeteries provide a useful service?
3 Would you be willing to spend a large amount of money to have a pet buried?
4 How are most dead pets disposed of?
5 Do you think giving animals a funeral is sentimental rubbish?
6 Greyfriars Bobby and Hachiko were both faithful to their masters and waited years for them. Is that a sign of intelligence?
7 Do you think that the Dog Walk of Fame is a good idea? What is the real purpose of the memorial?
8 Do you recognise all the inductees of the first list? Would you add any dogs to it?

18 Blind ambition

Richard E Byrd became famous in 1926 when he claimed that he had navigated a plane to the North Pole. This achievement for which he was awarded the American Congressional Medal of Honour marked the beginning of a very successful career.

-In 1827 with three companions he flew the Atlantic from west to east.

-In 1928 he led an expedition to the Antarctic and named the territory he visited Marie Byrd Land for his wife.

-In 1929 he flew to the South Pole with three companions.

-He played an important part in the Pacific during World War 2.

-When he died in 1957 he was an international hero.

Byrd had several reasons for wanting to reach the Pole; when he arrived in King's Bay, Spitzbergen, he found the Norwegian explorer Roald Amundsen making plans to fly to the Pole in an airship. Byrd had to be first to the Pole because:

-He had invested $20,000 in the trip;

-He had newspaper contracts and he had been sponsored by the National Geographic Society;

-All eyes from President Coolidge down were upon him.

When he announced that he was the first man to fly to the Pole a wave of pride swept the States; he had taken the first step of a magnificent career.

Hoax

Byrd did not reach the Pole because:

-He could not have flown from King's Bay to the Pole and back in 15 hours.

-Bernt Balchen who flew with him on his triumphal tour of the States said Byrd did not complete the 1,500 mile trip.

-Soon after take-off, the plane developed an oil leak so Byrd circled round and round out of sight and sound of King's Bay until he thought sufficient time had elapsed to support the story of having flown to the Pole.

-Byrd had a co-pilot, Floyd Bennett, on the flight; Balchen says that, just before he died,

Bennett revealed the details of the hoax: 'We were just north of Spitzbergen when the commander discovered the oil leak. He became quite concerned and ordered me to fly back and forth; finally he ordered me to return to King's Bay.

Donald Crowhurst

Many strange things have happened to competitors in single-handed yacht races. One spotted a baby elephant in the sea; it changed into a car and finally turned out to be a whale. One contestant saw his father-in-law at the top of the mast and another saw his wife, mother and daughter in his cabin. These delusions are quite amusing but the stress of single-handed sailing can turn to tragedy.

In 1969 Donald Crowhurst was a British businessman and amateur sailor who died while competing in the Sunday Times Golden Globe Race. He had entered the race in hopes of winning a cash prize to aid his failing business. Instead he encountered difficulties early in the voyage and secretly abandoned the race while reporting false positions in an attempt to appear to complete a circumnavigation without actually circling the Globe. Evidence found after he disappeared indicated that the attempt ended in insanity and suicide.

His background

-Crowhurst, a weekend sailor, designed and built a radio direction finder. While he did have some success in selling his equipment, his business began to fail.

-In an effort to gain publicity he tried to obtain sponsors to enter the Sunday Times race.

-His main sponsor was an English entrepreneur, Stanley Best, who invested heavily in Crowhurst's failing business.

-Once committed to the race, Crowhurst leveraged both his business and his home against Best's continued financial support.

-His financial situation was very bad.

-He had to win the race.

Questions

1 Byrd had a very successful career. Would it have been the same if the hoax had been discovered?

2 Byrd had a co-pilot, Floyd Bennett. Why did he keep quiet about Byrd's claim?

3 Why would Byrd claim he had reached the Pole when he hadn't?

4 Was Donald Crowhurst an experienced sailor? Why did he enter such a hazardous race?

5 Compare the two men's lives.

19 Record breakers

In 2010 blind ambition drove younger and younger boys and girls to undertake the most difficult tasks; here is a sample:

Jessica sails round the world

Tens of thousands of people welcomed 16 year old Jessica Watson, the youngest person to sail unassisted around the world, when she crossed the finish line at Sydney Harbour yesterday. The Australian teenager spent seven months at sea in her 34ft pink yacht, during which she battled 49ft waves, homesickness and critics who said she would never make it home. Prime minister, Kevin Rudd called her 'Australia's newest hero', a description she dismissed: 'I'm just an ordinary girl who believed in her dream.'

Jordan, 13, climbs Everest

Jordan Romero, a 13 year old American boy has become the youngest person to reach the summit of Mount Everest. He was accompanied by his father and three Sherpa guides. He has now climbed the highest mountains on six continents:

-2007 Elbrus in Europe
-2007 Aconcagua in South America
-2008 Kilimanjaro in Africa
-2009 Denali in North America
-2009 Carstensz Pyramid in Oceania
-2010 Everest in Asia

Before he left for Everest, his mother said he would do some schoolwork on the trip.

Bonita almost dies on Everest

Bonita Norris, 22, became the youngest British woman to climb Everest and almost died in the attempt. She slipped on the descent and had to be carried by Sherpas and her support team part of the way down the mountain.

Inevitably

A British climber collapsed and died hours after achieving his lifelong ambition of climbing Mount Everest. Peter Kinloch suffered blindness and began to stumble shortly after beginning his descent. Three Sherpas and the team leader stayed with him for twelve hours to administer drugs and oxygen in an effort to get him down, but were finally forced to abandon him at 8,600m because of worsening weather conditions.

Marathon cheats

-In June 1960, 69 year old Anthony Gaskell was due to receive a plaque after running the fastest time by a pensioner in the London Marathon. He will not now be honoured after it emerged that he had taken a short cut during the race, climbing over a barrier where the course doubled back on itself at Tower Bridge and cutting out 10 miles.

- In January 2010 a third of the top hundred finishers in the Xiamen Marathon in China were disqualified for, among other things, travelling sections of the race by car and hiring people to run in their place.

-Rosie Ruiz was the first woman to cross the line in the 1980 Boston Marathon: she caught a subway train and only ran the last mile.

Questions

1 Is Jessica Watson just an ordinary girl?

2 Do ordinary girls sail solo round the world?

3 Jordan Romero has spent a lot of time climbing mountains. Do you think he did much schoolwork on his expeditions?

4 Bonita Norris is lucky to be alive. How did she get down Everest?

5 Peter Kinloch was not so lucky. Why?

6 Why do people cheat in marathons? Do they benefit from their cheating?

7 Have you any ambition to climb Everest or sail solo round the world? What would you need to do either of these things?

20 Fame is the spur

In 1873, Matthew Webb was serving as captain of a steamship when he read an account of a failed attempt to swim the English Channel. He decided to try himself and gave up his job to train, first in Lambeth Baths and then in the Thames and the English Channel. His first attempt on August 12 1875 failed, but 12 days later he dived from the Admiralty Pier at Dover. Smeared with porpoise oil and accompanied by three boats he reached France in 21 hours 45 minutes. The rewards followed:

-He licensed his name for merchandising
-He wrote a book *The Art of Swimming*
-A brand of matches was named after him
-He gave swimming exhibitions
-He took part in stunts such as floating in a tank for 128 hours

Captain Webb's final stunt was to attempt to swim through the Whirlpool Rapids below Niagara Falls. He failed to raise sponsorship money but on 24 July 1883 he jumped from a boat near the suspension bridge. He survived the first part of his swim but drowned near the entrance to the Whirlpool. In 1909, a memorial was unveiled in Dawley, his home town; the inscription read: 'Nothing great is easy.'

After Webb, the deluge

Since Captain Webb swam the Channel there have been 948 successful crossings. The Queen of the English Channel is Alison Streeter; she has made 43 crossings and her fastest time is 8 hours 48 minutes.

Francis Chichester

He arrived in Plymouth in his yacht Gypsy Moth 1V after completing his epic single-handed voyage around the world. He crossed the finishing line nine months and one day after setting off from the historic port. Sir Francis is the first man to sail round the world solo with only one port of call, Sydney.

Chichester's single-handed voyage inspired the Golden Globe Race. The considerable publicity to which his achievement gave rise led a number of sailors to plan the next logical step – a non-stop single-handed round the world sail.

The Sunday Times had sponsored Chichester with highly profitable results and was interested in being involved with the first non-stop circumnavigation; but they had the problem of not knowing which sailor to sponsor. They solved this by declaring the race open to all comers, with automatic entry. This was in contrast with other races of the time for which entrants were required to demonstrate their single-handed sailing ability prior to entry.

Inspiration

The example set by Francis Chichester inspired many a sailor to follow him. Since there weren't any obstacles to prevent anyone who wished to sail round the world from doing so, many tried their skills and their luck. They weren't deterred by the tragic fate of Donald Crowhurst and the sailors got younger and younger.

Between 1996 and 2010 seven sailors of 21 years of age or younger completed the single-handed circumnavigation. Mike Perham was 17 years 164 days; Zac Sunderland was 17 years 229 days; Zac's sister was 16 when she set off on a solo sail on 23 January 2010: she went missing on 11 June. This set off a costly air and sea search which involved an Airbus A330 search plane and four boats. It was a French fishing boat which eventually rescued her.

During the rescue the captain of the boat fell overboard and had to be rescued from the rough sea.

A step too far

A Dutch teenager Laura Decker was 14 when she announced her plan to sail solo round the world. This was too much for the Dutch law and a court blocked her bid. This was too much for Laura who disappeared and was found safe and sound in the Dutch Antilles island of St Maarten.

Laura at 14 is a seasoned sailor who was born on a yacht off the coast of New Zealand during a seven year world trip. She had a yacht by the age of six and began sailing solo when she was ten. Her father supports her attempt on the record while her mother has expressed some doubts.

The best-laid plans

Dan Martin, an unemployed teacher is planning a global triathlon. He intends to:
-swim the Atlantic, which will take four to six months;

-cycle from France to the east coast of Russia which will take quite a long time if he gets a puncture;
- run a marathon a day to New York.

The estimated cost of £200,000 will be met by corporate sponsors. Any donations will go to the Dan Martin Foundation, his own charity for under-privileged children.

In June 2010 the global triathlon was postponed due to lack of sponsorship cash.

Questions

1 Do you agree with Captain Webb's epitaph: Nothing is too easy?
2 What motivated Webb to take the huge risk of swimming the Whirlpool Rapids?
3 So far, Alison Streeter has made 43 Channel crossings. Why does she do it?
4 Why do you think Chichester, who was not a young man, undertook to sail solo round the world?
5 Was it a good idea to open the Golden Globe Race to all comers?

6 What did the rescue of Abby Sunderland entail? Who paid for it?

7 Was the Dutch court right in preventing Laura Decker from setting off on a solo round the world trip?

21 Playing the triangle

Frank Edwards an American broadcaster used to present a programme called *Stranger than Science* which was about unsolved mysteries. When in 1959 he published a book with the same title he said that one of his aims was 'to solve the mystery of whether an author could make money out of a book like this.' It became a best-seller.

Fifteen years later Charles Berlitz developed one of the mysteries from *Stranger then Science* and called it *The Bermuda Triangle*; it too became best-seller. Here is an extract from Frank Edwards' original story.

In a comparatively small area off the south-east coast of the United States more than a score of modern planes have vanished without a trace, carrying crews and passengers to oblivion. The mysterious loss of all these lives in this one area has earned it the ominous title: *Point of no Return.*

Edwards goes on to tell the story of five Avenger torpedo bombers which disappeared without trace in 1945. From his account the pilots got lost, ran out of fuel and crashed into the sea; being made of metal, the planes sank and communications stopped.

In November 1975 *Horoscope Magazine* carried an article: Can astrology solve the Bermuda Triangle mystery? It retold the story of the five Avengers and decided that the answer to the mystery was to be found in the stars. Here is an *extract:*

Much has been made of the simultaneous failure of the instruments on board the vanished planes. It has been suggested that the submerged mythical Atlantis carried with it powerful atomic piles which today exert disturbing influences on sensitive instruments. This suggests rather the changing planetary patterns which as we know do affect radio and similar devices.

Don't believe everything you read

In the same year Larry Kuche wrote in the magazine *Fate*: In almost all the supposed mysterious losses within the Triangle good hard research shows that the facts as originally presented are inaccurate. In some cases they have been deliberately falsified. Yet few readers have thought to question this information. Despite the warning, 'Don't believe everything you read' most readers do believe just about everything they see in print.

The last word?

In a letter to *Horoscope,* Lloyds the ship and aircraft insurers said: According to Lloyds' records 428 vessels have been reported missing throughout the world since 1955 and it may interest you to know that our intelligence service can find no evidence to support the claim that the Bermuda Triangle has more losses than elsewhere.

Still going strong

Thirty-five years after the Lloyds letter was sent the Bermuda Triangle is still being talked and written about.

Here is an extract from a BBC programme broadcast in 2010:

Bermuda Triangle mystery solved

Scores of ships and planes are said to have vanished without trace in the vast triangular area of ocean with imaginary points in Bermuda, Florida and Puerto Rico. But Tom Mangold's new examination for the BBC provides plausible explanations for the disappearance of two British commercial planes in the area with the loss of 51 passengers and crew.

One plane probably suffered from a catastrophic failure as a result of poor design while the other is likely to have run out of fuel. At the time commercial flights from London to Bermuda were new and perilous. It would require a fuelling stop in the Azores before the 2,000 mile flight to Bermuda, which at that time was the longest non-stop commercial overseas flight in the world.

The official investigation report on the disappearance of the first plane mused: 'some external cause may have overwhelmed both man and machine'. This comment may have opened the floodgates for conspiracy theorists, hack journalists and mischief makers, adding to the mystery of the Bermuda Triangle.

Questions

1 Why would a book about unsolved mysteries become a best seller?
2 Why did Charles Berlitz develop the Bermuda Triangle story?
3 Why was there no trace of the crashed Avengers? Is the Atlantis theory credible?
4 Is 'Don't believe everything you read.' good advice?
5 Why is the Lloyds letter to *Horoscope Magazine* decisive in solving the mystery?
6 Did the BBC programme really solve the mystery?

22 So unbelievable

Uri Geller is handsome, famous and rich but success has not turned his head as this modest dedication of his autobiography *My Story* reveals:

'This book is dedicated to those who have worked, contributed and loved for the past two and a half years and especially to my mother and father who devoted all their efforts and energies to bringing me up into something so unbelievable and so unknown.'

In 1975 many people were convinced the Geller was, as he claimed, a channel for some kind of supernatural force. Reports like *Uri's Bender* were common. Like Noel Gordon, a TV star, many people thought that 'there might be something in the things he does'. Professor John Taylor, a mathematician at the University of London, was convinced that Geller had supernatural powers.

Uri's Bender

Show jumper Amanda Metcalf was a bit upset with fork bender Uri Geller. She watched him go through his TV act at her home and three of the silver cups she had won bent at the stem.

Believing in Geller

Noel Gordon wrote: 'I don't think I should say much about Mr Geller as I have never seen him, but from the things I have heard and read there might be something in the things he does; but then, I do believe in extra-sensory perception.

Challenge to science

'The Geller effect of metal bending is clearly not brought about by fraud. It is so exceptional that it presents a crucial challenge to modern science and could even destroy the latter if no explanation became available' – Professor John Taylor

Just like that!

In his autobiography Uri Geller gave details of some of his supernatural experiences:

-He was teleported 36 miles across New York in an instant.

-His tape recorder had a habit of switching itself on and recording messages from outer space. The messages erased themselves once they had been played back. Geller wrote the messages down but they were a meaningless string of words.

-His camera levitated while he was on a flight (in a plane this time) so he took several shots through the window. Although he saw nothing, the film, when developed, revealed pictures of flying saucers.

Still bent

Uri Geller is still a first class illusionist and entertainer; he has a lucrative career as a motivational speaker: for a large fee he will entertain employees and motivate them to make lots of money for their companies; he is a past master at money making after all. His claims to fame are many; he still demonstrates his magical powers: he bends large amounts of cutlery; he has a Cadillac encrusted with about 5,000 pieces of cutlery riveted to the car. He bent some of the cutlery with brain power but the rest was shaped by a sculptor friend.

-He is the most investigated and celebrated exponent of the paranormal.

-He has worked for the FBI and CIA using mind power to erase Russian computer files and track serial killers.

-He has attended nuclear disarmament negotiations to bombard and influence delegates with positive thought waves so that they would sign the Nuclear Arms Reduction Treaty.

-He has used his gifts to successfully detect oil and precious metals.

-He is the motivational mind-power coach to Premier League footballers, industrialists, Formula One drivers and Olympic ice-skaters, boxers and cyclists.

The last word

In 1975 the science correspondent of the *Times Educational Supplement* regarded Geller as an entertainer. He thought the readiness of people to believe that he had supernatural powers was a sign of the troubled times, Here is an extract:

'The curious feature of the phenomenon of Gellerism is not of course Mr Geller himself but the eagerness of ordinary people to believe that what he does is indeed supernatural. It is of course an old habit: people who believe in ghosts, poltergeists and spirits are part of a tradition that goes back to the Middle Ages and beyond

Questions

1 Is Uri Geller a modest person?

2 Like Noel Gordon, do you think there may be something in Geller's claim to supernatural powers?

3 What really happened to Amanda Metcalf's three silver cups?

4 Professor Taylor believes that the Geller effect is clearly not brought about by fraud. Do you?

5 Can Geller fly like Superman?

6 Why did Geller have his Cadillac covered in bent cutlery?

7 What do you think of Geller's power to motivate people and influence their thinking?

8 Why are people ready to believe that Geller has supernatural powers?

23 Witches

We don't conduct witch-hunts anymore; the classical period for witch-hunts was between 1480 and 1700 resulting in an estimated 40,000 to 100,000 executions.

The Pendle Witches

The trials of the Pendle Witches in 1612 are the most famous witch trials in English history. The twelve people accused of witchcraft lived around Pendle Hill in Lancashire. They were charged with the murder of ten people by the use of witchcraft. Of the nine women and two men who went on trial, ten were found guilty and executed by hanging and one was found not guilty. Six of the Pendle witches came from one family. The outbreak of witchcraft in Pendle may show the extent to which people could make a living by posing as witches. They used three methods:

1 Healing: even in the 21st century a number of faith healers make a good living.

2 Begging: if a witch asked for alms many people were too afraid to refuse.

3 Extortion: witches extracted money from people by threatening them with terrible consequences if they did not pay up.

The Salem Witches

In 1692, in the town of Salem, Massachusetts, 24 people were killed after being tried as witches; hundreds of others were accused of being witches and wizards but managed to escape the gallows. The witch hunt in Salem was the result of several factors:

1 The economy of the town was in a very bad state and the inhabitants could not understand why.

2 The town was the centre of many religious faiths and rivalry between the churches was very strong.

3 As in the 21st century there were lots of bored teenagers looking for mischief.

4 There were many personal jealousies among the towns-folk.

Someone had to take the blame for all this and the result was a horrendous witch-hunt.

Witchcraft now

One might think we live in a more enlightened age and that belief in witchcraft is a thing of the past. This is not so; here is an example of what is happening now:

Child witches in Africa

Evangelical pastors are helping to create a terrible new campaign of violence against young Nigerians. Children and babies branded as witches are being abandoned and even murdered while the preachers make money out of the fear of their parents and their communities.

The Beirut psychic

This is a report from *The Guardian* of 3 April 2010: A Lebanese man sentenced to death for witchcraft will not be beheaded next week as had been expected. Ali Sibat, a 49 year old father of five, made predictions on an Arab satellite TV channel from his home in Beirut. He was arrested on a pilgrimage to Medina by Saudi religious police and sentenced to death for witchcraft.

The Saudi justice system which is based on Sharia law does not clearly define the charge of witchcraft; Ali Sibat is one of the scores of people reportedly arrested every year for witchcraft or fortune telling.

Exorcism

Exorcism is the practice of evicting evil spirits by causing them to swear an oath. The term became prominent in early Christianity as the casting out of demons. An exorcist is often a member of a church or an individual thought to have special powers or skills. It is a lucrative practice in Nigeria where they seem to have a lot of witches.

The best known exorcist was Jesus who performed many miracles. On one occasion he came across a man possessed by multiple evil spirits. Jesus addressed the spirits saying: 'Out unclean spirit; come out of this man!' Mark reported the solution: Now there happened to be a large herd of pigs feeding on the hillside and the spirits begged him: 'Send us among the pigs and let us go into them.' He gave them leave and the unclean spirits came out and went into the pigs, and the herd of about two thousand rushed over the edge into the lake and were drowned.

Questions

1 Why did some people in Pendle pretend to be witches?
2 How can hard times affect people's behaviour?
3 Is witchcraft dead?
4 What are the reasons behind the African obsession with witches?
5 Are predicting the future and fortune telling example of witchcraft or fraud?

6 Why do some churches have exorcists?

24 Prediction

What the facts foretell

Futurology is the science of predicting the future. A futurologist studies the facts of what has happened in the past, what is happening in the present and then tries to calculate what will happen in the future.

Governments want to know, for example, how many new houses, schools, hospitals and roads to build. The futurologist tries to answer this kind of question. From the facts about population increase or decrease he can forecast how many people there will be in future years. This will allow government planners to decide what will be needed.

So many people

The world's population has increased; these are the facts:
-10,000 BC just after the end of the last ice-age: I million

- 0 AD at the birth of Jesus: 200 million
- 1,000 AD the population doubles to 400 million
- 2010 AD the population increases almost seventeen-fold to about 7,000 million

This population explosion is causing concern about:

-Food production: how can we grow enough food to feed the world?
- Water shortage: how can we provide water for so many people and agriculture?
- Energy shortage: how can we power industries and buildings?

What the *Hotspur* foretold

In 1936 the *Hotspur* comic had an edition called *At school in 1975*. This predicted:

-There are no teachers; all teaching is done by television.
- All meals are scientifically prepared and served.
- Boys no longer play games on holiday but go on trips in their gyroplanes.

Among all this there is one man (the teacher) who sighs for the good old days of 1936.

Miscalculations

Very often futurologists are wrong; predictions about scientific advances can be wrong. For example:

-In 1906 scientists were agreed that aeroplanes would never fly long distances. Thirteen years later, Alcock and Brown flew a biplane across the Atlantic.

- In 1934 the British government said jet engines would never replace propeller driven engines. Seven years later the first jet plane flew.

- In 1949 most scientists agreed that space travel was impossible. Twenty years later the first men landed on the moon.

What the stars foretell

Astrology is an ancient branch of learning which is still taken seriously by a few people. Astrologers make predictions about what will happen to people, especially important people. In 1965 Jeane Dixon a famous American astrologer said:

-President Nixon has excellent vibrations and will serve his country well. Ten years later he retired in disgrace.

-Russia will be the first to put a man on the moon. Four years later the first man on the moon was an American.

A more enlightened age?

In 2010 astrologers are still making a good living from predicting the future. Many newspapers and magazines include horoscopes. Most people think of them as just innocent furn. Hundreds have predicted the end of the world and were careless enough to put a specific date on the event; here is just a selection.

-William Miller the founder of the Adventist Church predicted that the event would occur before 21 March 1844.Then he picked 18 April 1844; one of his followers suggested 22 October 1844.

-Jehovah's Witnesses expected Armageddon to arrive in 1975. In 1974 Witnesses were commended for selling their homes and property to finish out the rest of their days in full-time preaching. Oops!

-Harold Camping has an organisation which carries out evangelical work. He was convinced that the world would end in 2011 and said so in his broadcasts. In the meantime he continued accepting donations from the faithful. The world ended for Camping in 2013 when he died.

Saving the planet

In 1975 there was no mention of global warming; now it is constantly discussed. In the absence of Armageddon many scientists are preoccupied with forecasting the results of global warming. Here are some possible consequences:

-In 20 years average temperatures will be 2-3 degrees Celsius higher.

-Sea levels will rise as glaciers melt.

-Extreme weather events such as hurricanes and floods will be more frequent.

-More species will become extinct as the oceans warm.

-Human health will be affected by an increase in insect-borne diseases such as malaria.

Not everyone agrees with the above predictions. Global warming deniers say any rise in temperatures is part of a normal weather cycle and not produced by human activity. Whichever side of the argument you support it's only common sense to stop polluting the air with carbon dioxide.

Questions

1 Why is it important to predict the future?
2 Are there too many people on Earth?
3 Does everyone have enough food, water and energy at the moment?
4 Have any of the *Hotspur* predictions come true?
5 Do scientists today believe man will travel to the other planets?
6 Is astrology a useful science?
7 Why have so many people given a date for the end of the world?
8 Should we accept global warming as a fact? Why?

www.ingramcontent.com/pod-product-compliance
Lightning Source LLC
Chambersburg PA
CBHW060413290526
45791CB00002B/733